SMELLING
&
SELLING

BY: PAUL SHEETS

Smelling & Selling

Contents

Prelude

Why is it that women love perfume as much as men love cars? There are some researchers who believe that a woman's reason for loving perfume is because of the pheromones their bodies produce. Often, certain scents or perfumes trigger the increase of how much pheromone a woman's body will produce.

While a perfume will help in increasing the production of a woman's pheromone levels, they are also liked by women because of the attention they get from a member of the opposite sex or even from another woman.

In studies carried out, nearly 80% of all women will make a perfume purchase at least once each year.

Many women will tell you that the reason they purchase a particular perfume for themselves is that it makes them smell great and they seem to feel better about themselves. It also makes them feel a little bit more feminine.

Not only does smelling great make a woman feel good about herself, but it will make her feel attractive also.

Paul Sheets

In this book, we will be looking at ways of how to make your own perfume so that you can produce a scent which is particular to you, and unlike any of those that you can buy either in store or over the internet.

Perfume's History

People's use of scents, aromas and fragrances has been used for many centuries, and when and why people started to prepare and use them seems lost to us. However, over the years, evidence has been found through archeological findings, as well as texts written by our ancestors, that has shown just how aromas were being used. In the very early civilizations, scented flowers and herbs were used by people to worship the Gods, and when burned, some of these plants would release strong aromas. Such scented fires became part of many religious rituals. In fact, you will find that many religions still use scented fires today.

Both the Assyrian's and Egyptians used scented oils. Because of this, the demand for the raw materials needed to produce both fragrances and remedies led to the discovering of new ways of extracting scents from the plants they used. Such techniques as pressing, decoction, pulverization and maceration were developed and mastered by both the Assyrian's and the Egyptians. They even made attempts at trying to produce essential oils by distillation.

Slowly, the use of perfumes spread to Greece, where not only were they used in religious ceremonies, but also for personal purposes as well. When the Romans saw what the Greeks were doing, they began to use fragrances even more lavishly. There are many manuscripts around describing the herbs which they brought from all over the world to produce the fragrances they used.

As the Roman Empire fell, so the use of aromas for personal use began to decline. However, during the Middle Ages, perfumes again were being used only in churches in Europe for religious ceremonies and to cover the stench caused by the many diseases which abounded at this time.

Then when trade with the Orient was reestablished at the beginning of the 13th Century, exotic flowers, herbs and spices became more readily available around Europe. Venice quickly became the center of the perfume trade. It was not long before perfumery soon spread to other European countries. The perfume trade then developed even further, as those returning from the crusades reintroduced perfume for personal use.

However by the late 18th Century, the synthetic material fragrance was being produced, and this was the beginning of perfumery in the modern age. Thus with the introduction of synthetics, perfumes would no longer be exclusively used by the rich and famous. Also, because synthetics were now being used to produce perfumes, they could now be made on a much larger scale, although naturals were still also being used to help soften the synthetics. Today, natural products still remain a very important part of the production of perfumes in modern formulations.

But today, more and more people are turning away from the industrial techniques of producing perfume, and preferring to make it themselves instead. But for many people making their own perfumes, not only is it easy to do, but it is also a great source of pleasure and fun for them.

How Is Perfume Made?

Any perfume you buy or make yourself is a chemical compound made from fragrant oils, aroma blends, fixatives and solvents, which produce a pleasant or attractive smell. Primarily women use perfume in order to smell nice if they are attending a special event, or to help attract a mate.

The composition of any perfume starts with base perfume oils, which are natural, animal or synthetic, and are then watered down with a solvent to make them light and applicable. Unfortunately, perfume oils in either pure or undiluted form, can cause damage to skin, or an allergic reaction, so the adding of solvent is necessary to make them less potent. The most prevalent solvent used in the manufacturing of perfumes is Ethanol.

Paul Sheets

Plants are the oldest source for obtaining fragrant oil compounds from, and the parts used the most are the flowers and blossoms. But other plant parts, which can also be considered for use in perfume making, are leave, twigs, roots, rhizomes, bulbs, seeds, fruit, wood, bark and lichens.

As for perfumes which have been made using animal sources, they are normally made from Musk, and it is obtained from either the Asian Musk Deer or Civets (known as Civet Musk), as well as Ambergris (a fatty compound). Some perfume makers may also use either Castoreum or Honeycomb in the production of their perfumes.

As for synthetic source perfumes, these are produced through organic synthesis of multiple chemical compounds, and such things as Calone, Linalool, Coumarin and Terpenes are used to make synthetic fragrant oils. By using synthetic products in perfume making, you can produce smells which are both unnatural, and which may not even exist in nature, have become very valuable element in the making of perfumes nowadays.

Perfumes are made in order to attract the customer via the olfactory system (sense of smell) in order to persuade people to buy the perfumes or perfume laced products that they are producing.

A perfume composition will either be used to

augment other products, or patented and sold as a perfume after it has been allowed to age for one year.

Unfortunately, fragrance compounds will, after time, begin to deteriorate and lose strength if stored incorrectly. It is therefore important when thinking about making your own perfume, that you store them in tightly sealed containers, and keep them out of light and away from heat, as well as away from oxygen and other organic substances. If you want to get the best results possible the containers should be stored in a fridge at a temperature of between 3 and 7 degrees Celsius.

Today more than ever, perfume is popular around the world because both its use and application continues to grow.

The First Steps

In this chapter of the book we will look at a few simple ways in which you can make your own perfume for next to nothing.

Research has shown that you can actually make a 100 bottles of perfume for less than $300, and then, if you want, sell them for up to $50 each.

Certainly some of the most profitable perfumes that are now available are ones which have not cost much to produce.

Paul Sheets

Previously when people were looking to produce their own perfume it was very difficult to find the ingredients, along with the packaging (bottles, spray nozzles and more). But this has all now changed due to the internet and being able to order things online. Today you will find that you can obtain the ingredients you need at a reasonable price, and have the order sent directly to your home address.

However, there are some things which you will need to remember before you commence making your own perfume, and some of these are shown below.

You first need to think of a name for your perfume (something catchy so people will remember it). Now you have the name, you need to design a label (simple artwork would be best).

Next you need to look at what kinds of ingredients you will require, and make a list.

Search for the best types of bottles, lids and pumps that you will need to put your perfume into (spend a little more on this item); you want your perfume to look good.

Then you will need to spend a couple of days choosing your fragrances. It is important that you carry out as much research as possible on any other ingredients that you should use.

When preparing the ingredients, it is important that you are in a sterile environment before pouring the perfume into the bottles you have chosen and bought.

Finally, look at a way in which you can present the finished product to customer it may be in a box, or you may find a much more creative way doing this.

As you can see producing your own perfume is a simple process and if it is something you have always considered doing then why not give it a go.

Making Your Own Perfume

Whether you have decided to make perfume for your own personal or family use, or as a gift for a loved one or friend, it is in fact something you can easily do by yourself or with others. Certainly producing your own perfume is not only a great way of learning a new skill, but it may also boost your confidence, and most importantly, you will have fun when doing it.

If you carry out a search on the internet on "making perfume", you will soon find there is a wealth of knowledge out there on the many ways and different recipes to make it. But the most important thing you should think about before making any decisions, is what sort of perfumes it is you would like as your finished product.

First, you need to consider what sort of perfume it is you would like to make? Would it be an eau de cologne, perfume concentrate or even an aftershave?

Secondly, you need to decide what it should smell like? Do you want it to be soft or strong, sweet or manly or unisex? Does it have to be long lasting?

Now that you have made a decision by answering the questions above as to what kind of perfume it is that you would like to make, you need to start making a list of the ingredients that you need. When making the list, you should think about the characteristics of the various ingredients that you want to include in your recipe. However, if you already have a recipe that you would like to use, it may mean you do not need to bother experimenting with the ingredients you have (it may be wise to adjust the quantities of the ingredients you are using in order to make the perfume more personalized). However, if you do not have your list of ingredients already prepared, then there are a couple things that you should know prior to making your list.

First, when making perfume it is important that you experiment as much as you can. It should be remembered that perfume making is an art, and imagination and a great sense of smell will help you to overcome any lack of knowledge or experience that you have.

The next most important thing in relation to perfume making is that there are 3 key ingredients you will need to produce perfume.

Essential Oils (these have been extracted from various plants (organic or non-organic)) and when combined give the smell of the perfume you are trying to produce.

    A. Pure Grain Oil

    B. Water

Also, another thing that you should know about in relation to oils used in perfumes, is that there are 3 different types of oils, and these will ultimately influence the smell of perfume over time.

The Base Oil (Base Notes) – This will produce the scent that stays longest on the skin and for this reason it is usually added to the mixture first.

The Middle Oil (Middle Notes) – This also influences the smell of the perfume for quite some time, but not as long as the base notes does.

Top Oils (Top Notes) – This is added to the mixture after the middle notes, and may then be followed by some other substance which will help to bridge the scents together.

It is very important that when you are making perfume, you mix the extracts in the above order, and that you use enough of each type (usually equal amounts) in order to produce the right sort of perfume.

Below are provided a list of oils that you can easily obtain and which will help you to produce the perfume of your dreams.

A. Base Notes – Sandalwood, Vanilla, Cinnamon, Mosses, Lichens, Ferns

B. Middle Notes – Lemon Grass, Geranium, Neroli, Ylang-Ylang

C. Top Notes – Orchid, Rose, Bergamot, Lavender, Lemon, Lime

Now that you have read the above and considered all the possibilities it is time to start making your own perfume.

Things You'll Need & Where To Obtain Them

Now that you have made a decision to produce your own perfume, whether to earn an extra income or just as a hobby, you will need to start looking for places where you can get your supplies from. So in this chapter of the book we will look at ways of getting the necessary supplies in order for you to make your own perfume.

1. First, you will need to choose a formulation or perfume recipe. The reasons perfumes differ is down to the formulation or recipe that has been used, and in order for you to produce a perfume that people will like, it is necessary to choose a good recipe or formulation.

It is very important that you decide what kind of perfume it is you want to make, and then read through the description of a particular recipe, to see if it will produce the desired result you are looking for.

2. Next, you will need to look at essential and fragrance oils that are available. As these are one of the major ingredients in the making of perfumes, it is important that you choose ones which are of a good quality. The better quality oils you use, the

better quality your finished product will be.

The oils used will establish the perfume's inherent attributes, like mood, quality and character. What you should remember, however, is that essential oils are much more expensive than fragrance oils. When first starting out, it may be wise to just use fragrance oils only to save on money until you've become more skilled.

Also it is important that you learn about, and understand, the health risks which are associated with essential and fragrance oils. There may be some formulations or recipes which could cause health problems if the oils included in them are used incorrectly.

3. Any perfume made today is not made with fragrance or essential oils alone, and alcohol is also used as the primary solvent (helps to reduce the strength of the oils).

4. When making any homemade perfume, it is important that you use the right materials for not just measuring, but for handling, mixing and storing the finished product in.

Do not use utensils you already have in your kitchen (ones for measuring water or food items), as they are not suitable for measuring fragrance oils, alcohol and other such solutions that are required to make perfume. It is better that you use measuring devices that allow you to exactly measure out the amounts of oils and solvents required. If you do not, the perfume you make may not be what you wanted. It is best if you use measuring devices made from glass so that you can see what is inside and when handling any formulas (i.e., transferring them to storage bottles or other containers), then use a funnel with a narrow long neck.

5. Fixatives are used with the other ingredients in order to lower the rate of evaporation of the fragrance or essential oils. The reason why a perfume may lose its fragrance faster than normal is because only a little amount of fixative was used when preparing the perfume.

Now that you know what supplies you need to use to make perfume, you need to know where to get them. You may be able to get them from a shop in your area. You could also go online, as there are plenty of places which sell perfume kits. Simply do a search for "perfume kits", and you will soon see what is available.

Making The Perfume

When making homemade perfumes as previously discussed, there are 3 main ingredients which you will need, and these are:

1. Essential Oils

2. Water

3. Alcohol

Many of these items can be either obtained from a store that specializes in such ingredients, or over the internet.

You will also need a large saucepan, large bowl (for mixing all the ingredients together), spoon and some measuring cups or jugs to make perfume at home.

Provided below, are a few easy recipes that you should be able to produce at home without too much hassle.

Basic Recipe:

All you need for this recipe is some water, chopped flower blossoms (use lilac or lavender if blossoms unavailable).

Place the flower blossoms in a bowl, add the

water and then cover them and leave them overnight. The next day, the solution can be put into small bottles and sprayed either into the air or on to your skin.

Amaze:

For this, you will need some distilled water, vodka, hypericum perforatum, cypress and rosemary (all of which are essential oils). They should then be mixed together and stored overnight.

After a period of 12 hours or more, the solution produced can be put into a dark spray bottle to be used. Using a dark colored bottle will help the solution to remain fresh, which will be felt by the person using it when they apply it to their skin.

Whispering Rain:

This is another recipe that may be worth trying out. Again, you will need distilled water, some vodka, Sandalwood, Bergamot and Cassis essential oils (which can also be purchased as fragrance oils).

These ingredients should be stirred together and then stored overnight in a covered container. Then, the next day, it can be transferred to a dark colored bottle. This perfume must be kept in a cool place so that it does not dry up.

The three perfumes above normally last for

about a month before they lose their scent and the next recipe should produce something a bit better.

For this recipe, you will need fragrance oils such as Sandalwood, Cedar Wood, Bergamot, Vodka and a little touch of Vanilla. All these ingredients should be put into a jar and then shaken. It should then be put in a cool place and left for a week. After this time, you can then transfer the mixture into small perfume bottles.

If you would like to learn more about recipes for making your own perfume, you could always do a search of the internet. I also recommend visiting your local bookstore, where they will have books on the subject.

It is important to remember that these types of perfume recipes only have a shelf life of a month, therefore you will need to make new batches every few weeks.

Aromatic Perfumes

Using essential oils to make your own perfume is not only great fun, but also extremely satisfying as well. Also, these natural perfumes can help to enhance a person's good mood, drive away a bad one, help them to relax or even to provide them with some energy. It may even make you feel glamorous, exotic, confident or utterly feminine as well.

The recipes provided below are simple to make and easy to follow, and all you need to do is choose which one you want to try. If you want you could do a search to see which essential oils blend well together and try them instead.

So, by following the simple instructions provided below, you will soon be making your very own aromatherapy perfume.

First, you need a base. It can either be alcohol or a carrier oil (but the best is a mixture of the two together). The best type of alcohol to use is one which is odorless (say vodka) and mix this with Jojoba, Jojoba is particularly good, as it has a long shelf life, and once it is put on the skin, it tends to dry out and leave a wonderful scent behind.

However, jojoba is one of the more expensive carrier oils, and I would suggest you experiment with one of the cheaper ones (such as almond or apricot kernel oil) instead. Then, once you are happy with the product you are producing, you can produce the same product but with jojoba oil instead.

The equipment you will need for making aromatherapy perfume is as follows:

1. Measuring Spoons (Any good kitchen store will have these)

2.   Small Funnel (Can be purchased at any good DIY or hardware store).

3.   Small Colored Bottles (Look around your local stores or carry out a search on the internet).

4.   Dropper (not all essential oil bottles have one of these included with them).

Now we will provide you with the instructions for producing your first batch of aromatherapy perfume.

1.   1 teaspoon of carrier oil (Jojoba, Almond or Apricot Kernel) and 1 teaspoon of alcohol (Vodka), and with the small funnel, place these in the bottle.

2.   Next, add the essential oils from your chosen recipe (below you will see a number of different recipes, with the quantities of essential oils you require for them). You may need to get a dropper, as not all essential oil bottles come with one, and add a drop at a time.

3.   After adding each drop of essential oil to the rest of the mixture, the bottle should be shaken (remember to put

the lid on first before shaking).

4.   Once you have finished adding the last drops of essential oil and shaken, make sure the lid is on tightly, and store in a cool dark place for 12 days or more. However, each day you should remember to give the bottles a shake at least 3 times.

5.   After 12 days you can begin to enjoy the aromatherapy perfume that you have made.

The first recipe below is specifically for those women who may suffer from nerves on their wedding day, and will help to feel much more relaxed and calm on their big day.

All you need to make this recipe is:-

a.   4 drops Jasmine

b.   2 drops Lemon

c.   1 drop Patchouli

The following recipes have been designed to help produce a much more calming effect to the person using them. These perfumes will help to focus you on your inner self, and provide you with a feeling of security, which will promote a feeling of total relaxation.

Tranquility:

4 drops of Cedar wood

2 drops of Clary Sage

1 drop of Grapefruit

2 drops of Mandarin

Chill Out:

2 drops of Grapefruit

2 drops of Patchouli

1 drop of Rose

3 drops of Vetivert

2 drops of Ylang-Ylang

Sleep Tight:

2 drops of Bergamot

3 drops of Chamomile

2 drops of Marjoram

4 drops of Lavender

Silence:

3 drops of lavender

3 drops of Neroli

2 drops of Spearmint

The next recipes we are looking at will enhance a person's mood and feelings of wellbeing. These perfumes will help to relax and surround you with warmth, as well as a feeling of pure luxury for those special nights out or at home with your loved one.

Ardour:

3 drops of Jasmine

3 drops of Neroli

4 drops of Orange

Devotion:

1 drop of Clary Sage

3 drops of Patchouli

2 drops of Rose

4 drops of Rosewood

Tenderness:

2 drops of Linden Blossom

3 drops of Lime

2 drops of Neroli

Paul Sheets

3 drops of Sandalwood

Zeal:

4 drops of Melissa

2 drops of Rose

2 drops of Ylang-Ylang

So now that you have a few recipes to consider, why not go out and purchase some ingredients and equipment today to start making your own aromatherapy perfumes!

Simple Recipes

In this chapter we will look at a number of different recipes, not just for perfumes, but colognes and body sprays as well, which can easily be made in your own home.

The first recipe we will be looking at is the basic perfume recipe. This is the simplest of all perfume recipes that you can reproduce at home.

The ingredients you need are as follows:

1. 2 cups of water

2. 2 cup fresh chopped flower blossoms (you may want to use such flowers as lavender,

lilac, orange blossoms or honeysuckle).

Directions:

In a bowl, put a cheesecloth (make sure that the edges of the cloth hang over the side of the bowl). Fill this with 1 cup of flower blossoms (you choose) and then pour water over them until they are completely covered.

Cover the bowl and allow it to sit overnight. The following day, take hold of the edges of the cheesecloth hanging over the side of the bowl and lift it up, then gently squeeze the scented water produced into a small pot. You will now need to place this water into a pot and allow it to simmer until there is about 1 teaspoon left of the liquid. Allow the solution to cool, and place it in a small bottle. Perfume made this way normally has a shelf life of about 1 month.

The following recipes are all as easy to make as the basic recipe, but they will all be a little more fragrant because of the ingredients used. They also include either essential or fragrance oils as part of the recipe.

The first will bring the smell of the orient to you.

Ingredients:

Paul Sheets

4 drops of Sandalwood

4 drops of Musk

3 drops of Frankincense

2 teaspoons of Jojoba oil (carrier oil to be used when using essential or fragrance oils in perfume making).

Directions

Mix all of the ingredients together in a bottle and shake well.

Place them in a dark colored bottle, and then allow the perfume to settle for at least 12 hours.

Once it has been stood for 12 hours or more, you should now store it in a cool dry area.

The next recipe is also simple to make, but uses not only essential/fragrance oils, but also water and alcohol, as previously mentioned in this book.

Ingredients:

2 cups distilled water

3 tablespoons of Vodka

5 drops of Lavender

10 drops of Chamomile

10 drops of Valerian

Directions:

Mix all these ingredients together in a bottle and shake it well.

Transfer the mixture to a dark colored bottle, and again, as with the previous recipe, allow the bottle to stand for 12 hours or more.

Once the bottle has stood for the recommended 12 hours, it can be used, and then stored in a cool dry area.

The next recipe we are looking at is in fact not a perfume, but a cologne, and contains lemon as the main ingredient.

Ingredients:

1 cup of distilled water

1 cup of Vodka

3 drops of Lemongrass

10 drops of Lavender

10 drops of Lime

Directions:

Combine the essential oils with the vodka in a

Paul Sheets

bottle and shake well.

Now set this aside for 3 weeks.

After 3 weeks, you will need to add the distilled water and then let it stand for a further week.

It is important that you shake the bottle once a day while it is standing over the 4 week period.

After 4 weeks, you can transfer the mixture to dark bottles for storage, or keep the mixture in the bottle it is in, in a dark cool place.

The final recipe provided below is one which will produce a body splash, rather than a perfume, and has a citrus aroma to it.

Ingredients:

2 cups of distilled water

3 tablespoons of vodka

1 tablespoon each of lemon and orange peel (which must have been finely chopped)

5 drops of Lemon Verbena

10 drops of Mandarin

10 drops of Orange

Directions:

Mix the fruit peels with the vodka in a jar, cover and let it stand for 1 week.

After the week, strain the liquid and add the essential oils and distilled water to it.

Now let the mixture stand for a further 2 weeks, and make sure you shake the jar well once a day during this time.

Place the final solution after the 2 weeks in a dark bottle(s), or keep it in a cool dark area.

As you can see making your own perfumes, colognes or body sprays is simple, and once you've made your first lot and tried it yourself, you will soon want to be making more.

Selling Your New Perfume

You have now begun to produce your home made perfume, and have decided not just to give it as gifts to your friends or family, but instead would like to sell it to a wider audience.

One of the first things you will need to look at when making the decision on selling your own perfume is what it will be called. You will then need to start looking for bottles into which you can put your finished perfume. Then you will need to design a label for inclusion on the bottle, and also the kind of packaging that you will present the perfume in.

When looking at what sort of bottles you are considering to place your finished product in, you might want to think about vintage perfume bottles (but make sure they have been thoroughly sterilized). They will certainly provide you with an individual look that cannot be found when buying perfumes that have been mass produced. Just take a wander around your local antique shops or bric-a-brac shop, and you will soon find a wealth of different perfume bottles that you could use.

The best place to start when you are considering selling your own perfume is to do a search on the internet. There are many sites and companies which will provide you with all the necessary information you need.

However, you should be warned that, when you decide to sell your own perfume, you will need to make some outlays in order to get the business started.

For instance, you will need to factor in such costs as the purchase of all the ingredients for making the perfume, and the bottles that you will be putting the finished product into. Other costs that you will have to pay out for are the production of the labels that will be affixed to your finished product's bottles, and the cost of the packaging that you will use.

When first selling your product, it is advisable that you keep a record of all of your outgoing expenses so that you can price your perfume accordingly. The usual pricing equation is to triple the price it has cost you to manufacture your product. So say it has cost you $5 to produce each bottle, you should probably sell it for at least $15.

One of the best ways of selling your own perfume is through word of mouth of friends and family. However, for a small outlay, you could actually set up your own website and sell it from there.

If you are not sure how to go about setting up a website, then by searching the internet you will soon find there are lots of people out there who are willing to help. There are even people who have set up sites which will not only help you to build your site, but also help with the marketing and promotion of the product you have to offer. Begin by doing a search on the internet and looking for "starting a small web business". You will soon find a whole list of sites that are willing to assist you.

So, as you can see, making perfume is not only easy but also is very profitable.

Smelling & Selling